LIGHTNING BOLT BOOKS™

Human-Like Robots

Lola Schaefer

Lerner Publications • Minneapolis

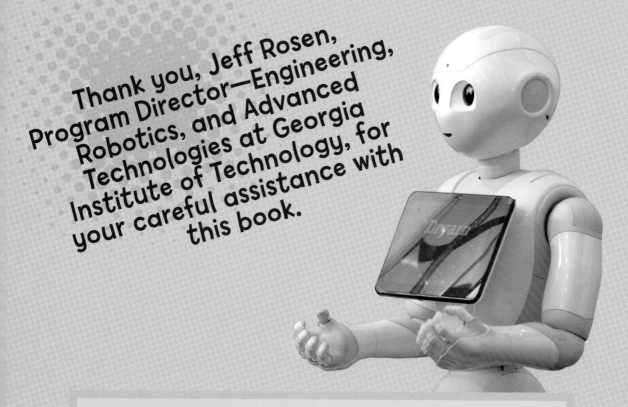

Thank you, Jeff Rosen, Program Director—Engineering, Robotics, and Advanced Technologies at Georgia Institute of Technology, for your careful assistance with this book.

Lerner Publications Company
An imprint of Lerner Publishing Group, Inc.
241 First Avenue North
Minneapolis, MN 55401 USA

For reading levels and more information, look up this title at www.lernerbooks.com.

Main body text set in Billy Infant regular.
Typeface provided by SparkType.

Editor: Alison Lorenz

Library of Congress Cataloging-in-Publication Data

The Cataloging-in-Publication Data for *Human-Like Robots* is on file at the Library of Congress.
ISBN 978-1-5415-9695-5 (lib. bdg.)
ISBN 978-1-72841-359-4 (pbk.)
ISBN 978-1-72840-044-0 (eb pdf)

Manufactured in the United States of America
1-47801-48241-1/24/2020

Table of Contents

What Are Human-Like Robots?

A robot directs traffic on a busy street. It waves cars along with hand motions. Sometimes it tells cars to stop.

At a 2017 robotics show in Rostov, Russia, visitors could talk to and play with robots.

Human-like robots do many jobs. A human-like robot has a head, body, arms, and legs. These robots can be large or small.

Robot limbs have joints so they can bend like human arms and legs do.

Many human-like robots have feet-like parts to walk, run, or kick a ball. Other human-like robots roll on wheels.

Most human-like robots have artificial intelligence (AI). AI helps the robots speak. It allows them to learn and solve problems.

Robots that learn are better at working with humans.

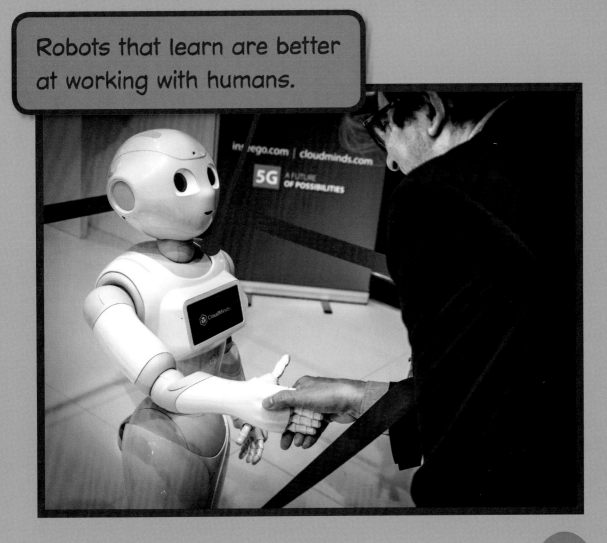

Human-Like Robot Parts

Most human-like robots have movable joints. They can move their heads left, right, up, and down. They can bend their bodies forward and backward.

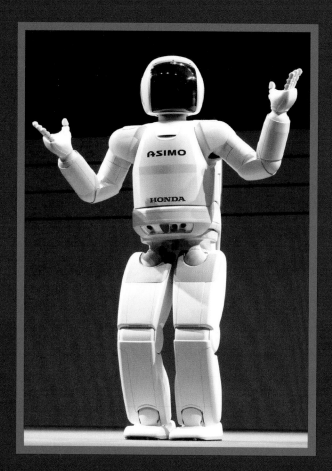

Many robots have hand-like grippers. These help the robots grab and lift objects. Some can even catch a ball.

Each human-like robot has the parts it needs to do a specific job.

The robots' eyes are sensors. The sensors send videos and photographs to the robots' computers. This information helps the robots move and speak.

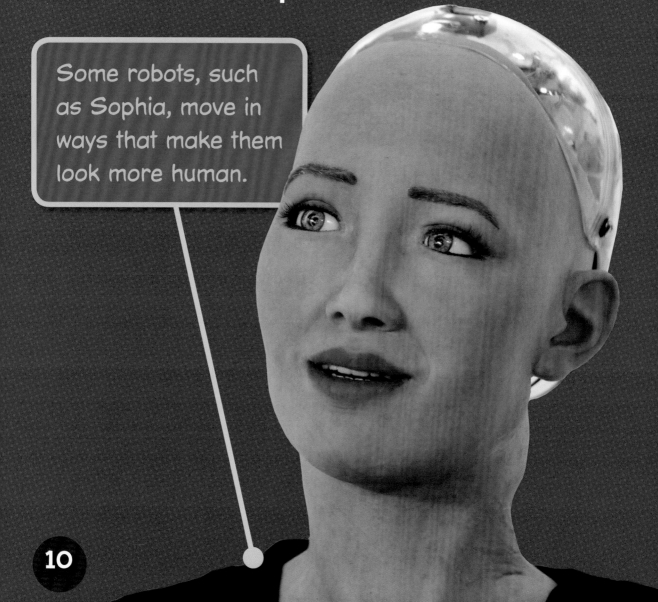

Some robots, such as Sophia, move in ways that make them look more human.

Human-like robots can think using computers. Engineers program the computers, or give them instructions to follow.

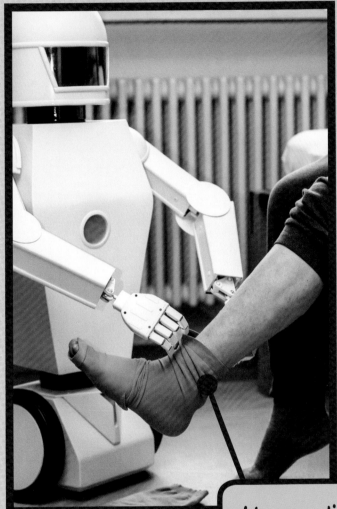

Human-like robots might follow instructions to help someone get dressed.

Robots at Work

Many businesses use human-like robots. The robots greet people. They are always polite and friendly.

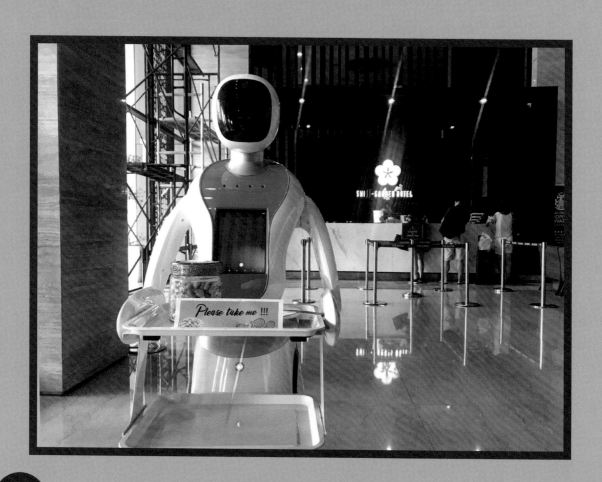

A robot server works at a café in Italy.

Some robots work in restaurants. They bring out food to customers. At the end of the meal, they clean the table for new guests.

In some restaurants, human-like robots make food in the kitchens. They can cut food into bite-size pieces.

This robot can make pancakes.

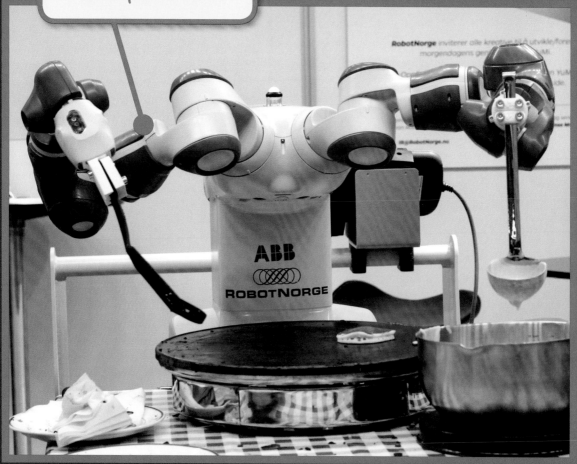

Human-like robots can help soldiers in the military. They can lift heavy supplies or carry hurt soldiers to safety. Someday, human-like robots may fight alongside soldiers in battle.

Rescue robots need to both lift heavy things and handle them gently.

Robots at Play

Some human-like robots can run as fast as 20 miles (32 kph) per hour. As they run, they can jump over objects in their way.

These robots can play sports. They can pass and catch balls. They can even play on teams!

Engineers want to build robots that can beat a human soccer team.

Human-like robots can juggle. The sensors in their eyes follow the balls. They never miss or drop a ball. These robots can juggle for hours!

Robots can do things for a long time without getting tired.

Robots can learn martial arts, such as karate or judo. Other robots can learn to dance. In the future, human-like robots will do more and more!

Imagine dancing with a big group of robots!

Behind the Robot

A human-like robot uses AI. The robot's sensors send data, or information, to its computer. The computer uses the information to tell the robot what it needs to say or do. For example, if the robot sees someone who looks sad, its sensors send that information to the computer. The computer then tells the robot to say, "Are you sad?"

Fun Facts

- In the future, human-like robots may care for children. These robots play games, help with homework, and speak to kids.

- Some robot faces were so human-like that they were scary. Newer robot faces look less human.

- Human-like robots work in senior centers. They talk to seniors and help them exercise.

- Police want to use more human-like robots. These robots could keep police officers out of dangerous situations.

Glossary

artificial intelligence (AI): a computer that copies human thinking

direct: to show someone the way to go

joint: a place where two or more parts meet and move

program: to give instructions to a computer

sensor: a device that can sense and record heat, size, shape, sound, or pressure

soldier: someone who is in the military

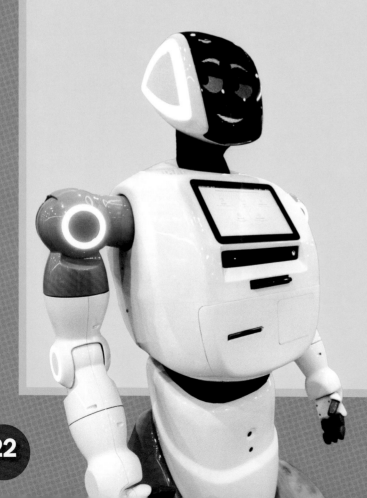

Further Reading

Furstinger, Nancy. *Helper Robots.* Minneapolis: Lerner Publications, 2015.

Robot Facts for Kids
https://kids.kiddle.co/Robot

Schaefer, Lola. *Robots on the Job.* Minneapolis: Lerner Publications, 2021.

Science Kids: Types of Robots
http://www.sciencekids.co.nz/sciencefacts/technology/typesofrobots.html

Science Trek: Robotics
https://sciencetrek.org/sciencetrek/topics/robots/

Silverstein, Rebecca. *The Robot Book.* New York: Children's Press, 2019.

Index

Photo Acknowledgments

Image credits: Antonello Marangi/Shutterstock.com, p. 2; Junior D. Kannah/AFP/Getty Images, p. 4; SergeyKlopotov/Shutterstock.com, p. 5; chabibur rochman/Shutterstock.com, p. 6; Paco Freire/SOPA Images/LightRocket/Getty Images, p. 7; Kyodo News Stills/Getty Images, p. 8; Tomohiro Ohsumi/Getty Images, p. 9; Anton Gvozdikov/Shutterstock.com, p. 10; Miriam Doerr Martin Frommherz/Shutterstock.com, p. 11; cypopcolour/Shutterstock.com, p. 12; Stefano Mazzola/Shutterstock.com, p. 13; elinba/Shutterstock.com, p. 14; U.S. Army/TATRC, p. 15; Mark Ralston/AFP/Getty Images, p. 16; Peter Parks/AFP/Getty Images, p. 17; Hiroshi Watanabe/Getty Images, p. 18; Tao Ke/Chengdu Economic Daily/Visual China Group/Getty Images, p. 19.

Cover: DeymosHR/Shutterstock.com.